JONAH, HABAKKUK & MALACHI

LIVING RESPONSIBLY

12 Studies for Individuals or Groups

MARGARET FROMER & SHARREL KEYES

SHAW

JONAH, HABAKKUK & MALACHI
A SHAW BOOK
PUBLISHED BY WATERBROOK PRESS
5446 North Academy Boulevard, Suite 200
Colorado Springs, CO 80918
A division of Random House, Inc.

Unless otherwise indicated, all Scripture quotations are taken from the *Holy Bible: New International Version* ® *NIV* ® Copyright © 1973, 1978, 1984 by International Bible Society. Used by permission of Zondervan Publishing House.

ISBN: 0-87788-432-3

SHAW and its circle of books logo are trademarks
of WaterBrook Press, a division of Random House, Inc.

Printed in the United States of America

03   02   01   00

10   9   8   7

CONTENTS

CONTENTS

INTRODUCTION

Near the end of the Old Testament are three little obscure prophetic books: Jonah, Habakkuk, and Malachi. These three prophets of Judah and Israel raised many questions that have always been a part of the human struggle. Though written hundreds of years before Christ, these books have startling relevance for Christians today.

Have you ever been troubled about the relationship between God's love and his justice? And what about the responsibility of an individual to his or her country versus the larger world scene? How should a Christian relate to the people of God around him? How much control can we expect to have over our own lives? How do we deal with the differences between God's perspective and ours?

These are some of the questions and issues faced head-on by Jonah, Habakkuk, and Malachi. In each book, we can sense the prophet's change of heart toward God as each gains a deeper understanding of God's sovereignty and what it means to live responsibly in God's sight.

God confronts his prophets (and through them, us) with the holiness of his character, the breadth of his perspective and love, and the quality of life he desires for his people. How did his people respond? How will we respond? That's what this study is all about.

HOW TO USE THIS STUDYGUIDE

Fisherman studyguides are based on the inductive approach to Bible study. Inductive study is discovery study; we discover what the Bible says as we ask questions about its content and search for answers. This is quite different from the process in which a teacher *tells* a group *about* the Bible and what it means and what to do about it. In inductive study God speaks directly to each of us through his Word.

A group functions best when a leader keeps the discussion on target, but this leader is neither the teacher nor the "answer person." A leader's responsibility is to *ask*—not *tell*. The answers come from the text itself as group members examine, discuss, and think together about the passage.

There are four kinds of questions in each study. The first is an *approach question*. Used before the Bible passage is read, this question breaks the ice and helps you focus on the topic of the Bible study. It begins to reveal where thoughts and feelings need to be transformed by Scripture.

Some of the earlier questions in each study are *observation questions* designed to help you find out basic facts—who, what, where, when, and how.

When you know what the Bible says you need to ask, *What does it mean?* These *interpretation questions* help you to discover the writer's basic message.

Application questions ask, *What does it mean to me?* They challenge you to live out the Scripture's life-transforming message.

Fisherman studyguides provide spaces between questions for jotting down responses and related questions you would like to raise in the group. Each group member should have a copy of the studyguide and may take a turn in leading the group.

A group should use any accurate, modern translation of the Bible such as the *New International Version,* the *New American Standard Bible,* the *Revised Standard Version,* the *New Jerusalem Bible,* or the *Good News Bible.* (Other translations or paraphrases of the Bible may be referred to when additional help is needed.) Bible commentaries should not be brought to a Bible study because they tend to dampen discussion and keep people from thinking for themselves.

SUGGESTIONS FOR GROUP LEADERS

1. Read and study the Bible passage thoroughly beforehand, grasping its themes and applying its teachings for yourself. Pray that the Holy Spirit will "guide you into truth" so that your leadership will guide others.

2. If the studyguide's questions ever seem ambiguous or unnatural to you, rephrase them, feeling free to add others that seem necessary to bring out the meaning of a verse.

3. Begin (and end) the study promptly. Start by asking someone to pray for God's help. Remember, the Holy Spirit is the teacher, not you!

4. Ask for volunteers to read the passages out loud.

5. As you ask the studyguide's questions in sequence, encourage everyone to participate in the discussion. If some are silent, ask, "What do you think, Heather?" or, "Dan, what can you add to that answer?" or suggest, "Let's have an answer from someone who hasn't spoken up yet."

6. If a question comes up that you can't answer, don't be afraid to admit that you're baffled! Assign the topic as a research project for someone to report on next week.

7. Keep the discussion moving and focused. Though tangents will inevitably be introduced, you can bring the discussion back to the topic at hand. Learn to pace the discussion so that you finish a study each session you meet.

8. Don't be afraid of silences: some questions take time to answer and some people need time to gather courage to speak. If silence persists, rephrase your question, but resist the temptation to answer it yourself.

9. If someone comes up with an answer that is clearly illogical or unbiblical, ask him or her for further clarification: "What verse suggests that to you?"

10. Discourage Bible-hopping and overuse of cross-references. Learn all you can from *this* passage, along with a few important references suggested in the studyguide.

11. Some questions are marked with a ♦. This indicates that further information is available in the Leader's Notes at the back of the guide.

12. For further information on getting a new Bible study group started and keeping it functioning effectively, read Gladys Hunt's *You Can Start a Bible Study Group* and *Pilgrims in Progress: Growing through Groups* by Jim and Carol Plueddemann.

SUGGESTIONS FOR GROUP MEMBERS

1. Learn and apply the following ground rules for effective Bible study. (If new members join the group later, review these guidelines with the whole group.)

2. Remember that your goal is to learn all that you can *from the Bible passage being studied.* Let it speak for itself without using Bible commentaries or other Bible passages. There is more than enough in each assigned passage to keep your group productively occupied for one session. Sticking to the passage saves the group from insecurity and confusion.

3. Avoid the temptation to bring up those fascinating tangents that don't really grow out of the passage you are discussing. If the topic is of common interest, you can bring it up later in informal conversation following the study. Meanwhile, help each other stick to the subject!

4. Encourage each other to participate. People remember best what they discover and verbalize for themselves. Some people are naturally shyer than others, or they may be afraid of making a mistake. If your discussion is free and friendly and you show real interest in what other group members think and feel, they will be more likely to speak up. Remember, the more people involved in a discussion, the richer it will be.

5. Guard yourself from answering too many questions or talking too much. Give others a chance to express themselves. If you are one who participates easily, discipline yourself by counting to ten before you open your mouth!

6. Make personal, honest applications and commit yourself to letting God's Word change you.

RUNNING AWAY

Jonah 1

Just about everyone knows the story of "Jonah and the whale." This tale of a reluctant prophet and a large fish captures our imagination, but put yourself in Jonah's place. Imagine being told to go preach on a street corner. Feeling uncomfortable? Now imagine being told to go preach on a street corner of a teeming urban center that is not only a huge seedbed of evil, but also the capital city of a powerful foreign enemy. Feeling more resistant?

This is just the situation Jonah faced, and he was uncomfortable. In this historical narrative of an incredible encounter between God, man, and nature, we see God's great concern and love for sinners everywhere.

1. What motivates you the most to share your faith with others?

♦ **Read Jonah 1.**

2. What did God tell Jonah to do, and why?

♦ **3.** What was Jonah's response? Why?

4. What might have been some of the positive and negative aspects of Jonah's assignment?

5. Why would any Christian want to flee from God's presence?

6. In what ways do you try to flee from God?

7. How did Jonah's response to God affect the people around him?

♦ **8.** What religious convictions did the sailors reveal by their actions?

9. What did Jonah believe about God?

10. How did his actions contradict his beliefs?

11. What do you know about God from this chapter?

12. In what ways do your actions and attitudes contradict your knowledge of God?

13. When you run away from God, what brings you back?

GETTING CAUGHT

Jonah 2

God's unique "rescue" of Jonah at sea by a huge fish was a strong reminder to Jonah that he could not flee from his responsibilities or from God's presence. Though this was a very desperate and lonely time for the prophet, God did not desert him. Frederick Buechner has observed, "No matter how deep the fish dove and no matter how dark the inside of its belly, no depth or darkness was enough to drown out the sound of Jonah's prayer."

1. Give some one-word impressions of what it would be like inside a great fish.

◆ **Read Jonah 2.**

2. What words and images describe Jonah's situation and his feelings about it?

3. What pressures (physical, emotional, and spiritual) would Jonah have been facing?

4. What alternatives to prayer do you use when you're in a tight spot?

5. Describe Jonah's attitudes toward himself, using chapters 1 and 2.

6. What do you think he learned about himself through his experiences on the ship and in the fish?

◆ **7.** How did Jonah's view of God appear to change during his prayer?

8. In this tough situation, what did Jonah find to be thankful for (verses 6-9)?

9. Jonah had acknowledged God all along. Why did he say, "I remembered you, LORD" (verse 7)? In what way had he forgotten God?

10. What evidence do we have that God had not forgotten Jonah (1:17; 2:10)?

11. What have you learned from Jonah about God's watching over his children?

12. Based on Jonah's experience, how might you pray for someone you love who is running away from God?

♦ **13.** God often uses not only catastrophes, but also the more common pressures of life to pull us back into a closer relationship with him. How has God used times of stress to draw you to him?

RESPONDING TO GOD

Jonah 3

Charles Spurgeon once said that "in our very worst case of despondency, we may still come to Jesus as sinners." God had caught Jonah red-handed in his disobedience, and offered him another chance. He also gave the rebellious people of Nineveh an opportunity to respond to his message. Seeing ourselves as we really are—sinners—is the first step in responding to God. This realization is our hope, for God's salvation is for sinners.

1. How do you know when you need to repent of sin in your life?

Read Jonah 3.

♦ **2.** Describe Nineveh as well as you can from this passage.

3. What was the difference in Jonah's response when the word of the Lord came to him this time?

4. How did the king describe what his people had been like? (Look for social strata, attitudes, actions, and reactions in verses 5-9.)

5. What evidence, if any, do you see that the people and their king knew they deserved God's judgment?

6. How did the people respond to Jonah's message? Include both attitudes and actions.

♦ **7.** What is involved in true repentance?

8. What are the differences between Jonah (in chapters 1 and 2) and the Ninevites (in chapter 3) in regard to:

a) their knowledge of God?

b) what they had to repent of?

c) their suggested motives for repentance?

d) their response to God's message?

9. Are you more like the Ninevites or more like Jonah in your response to God? Explain.

♦ **10.** How do you know God was more interested in their repentance than in their punishment (verses 9-10)?

11. Using the Ninevites as your model, what principles can you follow when someone exposes sin in your life?

12. Are there areas in your life in which you are resisting God? What changes do you need to make? Be specific.

SHOWING ANGER

Jonah 3:10–4:11

Have you ever been surprised at how God has helped someone who, in your opinion, really didn't deserve it? Have you ever resented the fact that God forgives and blesses "bad" people? These were some of the issues Jonah wrestled with as he saw God deal compassionately with his enemies. Sometimes it doesn't seem fair for people to be let off the hook. God doesn't always behave like we think he ought to, and, thankfully, though "man may dismiss compassion from his heart, God never will" (William Cowper).

1. How have you experienced God's compassion and grace in your life?

Read Jonah 3:10–4:11.

2. What words describe Jonah's attitudes toward God in chapter 4?

3. What were his reasons for being angry?

4. In what circumstances do you tend to be angry with God? Why? (Be specific.)

5. While Jonah was sitting outside the city, what were his chief concerns?

6. What was God concerned about?

◆ **7.** How did God use the plant to illustrate the rightness of his actions toward Nineveh?

8. What gaps have there been between Jonah's knowledge about God and his responses to God (see whole book)?

♦ **9.** Looking back over the whole book, list the ways in which God communicated to Jonah and directed his life.

10. When you need to know God's will, where might you expect to find it?

11. What does the book of Jonah suggest about how a person's relationship to God affects the people around him or her?

12. In what current situation or relationship is your concern not the same as God's?

LEARNING TO SEE WITH GOD'S PERSPECTIVE

Habakkuk 1:1–2:4

Judging from the headlines, it often seems that our world is reeling out of control. Wars rage between neighboring countries; violence is commonplace; innocent people are victimized; poor nations are oppressed by wealthy leaders. Will justice ever be done, or will wrong always have the upper hand? The prophet Habakkuk raised similar questions as he looked at the situation in his nation over two thousand years ago. And God shows that he was in control of history then, even as he is now.

1. How do you feel when you see evil win out over good?

♦ **Read Habakkuk 1:1-4.**

2. What did Habakkuk say were the problems in his country?

3. Imagine you are a citizen of Habakkuk's country. What would be hard about living there?

4. What was Habakkuk begging God to do when he questioned God in verses 1-3?

Read Habakkuk 1:5-17.

5. How did God say he would deal with the wickedness in Habakkuk's country?

6. Find all the words that describe the Babylonians (verses 6-11). What kind of people were they?

7. What additional information do we discover about the actions and character of the wicked (verses 14-16)?

What is the religion of the conquerors?

8. In spite of this oppression, what aspect of God's character did Habakkuk count on to preserve Israel (verses 12-13)?

What other question does Habakkuk raise?

9. Why is it sometimes hard to accept God's means of punishment?

10. What do you know about God that would help you in a seemingly unjust situation?

Read Habakkuk 2:1-4.

11. What did Habakkuk do to enable him to hear God's response?

♦ **12.** What did Habakkuk find out about the nature of God's word?

In what ways was God's answer a helpful one?

13. What can you do when you get tense over what God seems to be doing? (Review Habakkuk 1:1–2:4.)

LEARNING TO LIVE IN A MIXED-UP WORLD

Habakkuk 2:4-20

Habakkuk's world seemed in disarray with the strong and powerful lording it over the weak. But God let Habakkuk know that he was aware of the evil of the nations and revealed his judgment against them. As we learn to live in our mixed-up world today, we can take comfort in the old hymn that affirms: "This is my Father's world; O let me ne'er forget that though the wrong seems oft so strong, God is the ruler yet."

1. When have you been especially aware that God is in control of our world?

Read Habakkuk 2:4-5.

2. What are some character traits of the wicked person that God describes?

3. What needs is the wicked person trying to fulfill by his actions?

◆ **4.** How can living by faith protect you from these pitfalls?

Read Habakkuk 2:6-20.

◆ **5.** God showed Habakkuk five pictures of the wicked, each marked by a pronouncement of woe. For each section, answer the following questions:

a) What was their sins?

b) Can you suggest a modern-day equivalent for this sin?

c) What did God say would be their final end?

6. In what ways would the picture of God in verse 20 have been a comfort to Habakkuk?

7. What kind of social injustice are you aware of in your community?

What have you learned about God from this chapter that would help you correct these situations?

8. How do you feel when things seem to be going wrong all around you?

What have you learned from the book of Habakkuk that helps you?

◆ **9.** From this mixed-up world, briefly describe one situation in which you currently feel pressure. Pray together for each of these needs.

LEARNING TO REJOICE IN GOD'S SALVATION

Habakkuk 3

What is the foundation of your faith? Can you rejoice in God when things are difficult? In this closing prayer, Habakkuk remembers all God had done in the past for his people, and he chooses to trust God, no matter what his circumstances. Whether we live with plenty or in want, all we ultimately have to lean on is God, our Rock and our Salvation.

1. How has remembering what God has done for you in the past proved helpful in difficult situations?

◆ **Read Habakkuk 3:1-15.**

2. After having had several conversations with him, what was Habakkuk still calling on God to do (verse 2)?

◆ **3.** What evidence do you see that his tone had changed, although his basic request remained the same?

◆ **4.** Habakkuk's song contains a series of pictures of God acting in judgment. What images are most vivid to you?

◆ **5.** What were the results of God's actions?

For what purpose did he act?

6. What are some of the attributes of God revealed in this chapter?

How were these attributes displayed in what God had done for his people?

7. What has God done for you that makes you aware of these same attributes?

Read Habakkuk 3:16-19.

8. What was Habakkuk's response to this picture of fierce, holy wrath?

9. Why did he respond as he did?

10. As you become aware of God's holy wrath and your own sinfulness before him, what does the phrase "the righteous will live by his faith" (2:4) mean to you?

11. What would life be like if all of verse 17 were true at once?

12. How does Habakkuk's response in verses 18-19 illustrate what it means for the righteous to live by faith?

13. What are some differences between waiting for God to act and rejoicing in the Lord as you face difficult situations?

14. Are there any areas in your life in which God is calling you to live by faith right now?

WORSHIPING THE LORD ALMIGHTY

Malachi 1

Most of us treat our leaders, bosses, and people we admire with honor and respect. Why? Because of who they are and the position they hold. Yet how often do we enter God's presence disrespectfully and halfheartedly? This was Israel's problem. They had replaced their loving worship of God with a dry, empty, tired ritual. God confronted them about their sin and reminded them of who he really is.

1. What are some ways we show respect for leaders today?

♦ **Read Malachi 1:1-5.**

♦ **2.** Why did the Lord say he hated Esau and loved Jacob?

♦ **3.** Why was this hate for Esau a proof of his love for Jacob?

Read Malachi 1:6-14.

4. What evidence did God give that his own people did not love him?

5. What words can you find that show the extent of Israel's disaffection towards God?

6. What evidence from this chapter shows that God demands respect?

7. What does God want from his people?

8. In what areas of your life is there evidence of disrespect for God?

9. What are some consequences in your life when you cease to honor God?

10. In light of this passage, what one thing does God most desire from you right now?

LIVING IN FAITHFULNESS

Malachi 2:1-16

Mother Teresa was once asked if she felt her work among the poor in India was a success. She replied that she was not called to be successful, but to be faithful. Faithfulness is a hard quality to come by in a world that thrives on wealth, fame, and quick fixes. When promises are broken, marriage covenants disregarded, and employee burnout high, true loyalty and devotion to causes, relationships, or tasks is low. But we, as Judah of old, need to guard ourselves, listen to God's call, and not break faith with him.

1. What are some ways we show faithfulness today?

Read Malachi 2:1-9.

2. In what ways did God say he would punish the priests if they refused to take him seriously?

3. How did each of these punishments fit their sins?

◆ **4.** *Levi* in verse 4 stands for the priesthood. What kind of model was Levi for the priests who came after him?

Read Malachi 2:10-16.

5. Why would God have been particularly concerned with the actions and attitudes of the priests?

6. How were the sins of the priests reflected in the lives of the people of Judah?

7. Under what conditions is God displeased with our prayers and sacrifices? (Use both chapters 1 and 2.)

♦ **8.** In what ways are the covenant of marriage and a covenant with God similar?

♦ **9.** What does God desire from each covenant?

♦ **10.** Why does God hate divorce?

11. In what ways is it difficult to remain faithful to another person?

12. Using this passage, what leadership qualities would you look for in choosing Christian leaders for your church?

RETURNING TO GOD

Malachi 2:17–3:12

We see unjust suffering every day. Bad people seem to prosper; good people are innocent victims. It's natural to wonder where God is in the midst of injustice, and to want him to come and right all the wrongs. But God's justice always costs something. B. C. Forbes has observed that we may think we want justice, but what we want and need is God's mercy. When we return to God in repentance, we do not have to fear his justice.

1. What would you do if you knew the Lord was coming soon to establish justice?

Read Malachi 2:17–3:5.

2. What do you know about the messenger who is coming?

3. What would be the effects of being submitted to a refiner's fire?

4. If you wish, relate a time of hardship that has refined you and brought you closer to God.

5. In 2:17 the people asked, "Where is the God of justice?" What sequence of events would answer their question?

6. Sometimes we talk about God's justice as something negative, especially when it is applied to us. What positive aspects of God's justice can you draw from this passage?

Read Malachi 3:6-12.

7. What words and phrases reflect the people's attitude toward God?

8. What were the differences between the people's actions and attitudes and God's?

9. In what ways is it possible to rob God?

10. Why is it likely that if you have drifted away from God you are also robbing him?

♦ **11.** What is God longing to do for his people? (Use Malachi 2:17–3:12.)

12. With this in mind, what does God want to do for you right now?

What do you need to do to take advantage of God's generosity?

WAITING FOR HIS COMING

Malachi 3:13–4:6

Throughout this study God has addressed the questions and complaints of his people. He has dealt mercifully with those who turn to him. But he has also affirmed that he is the Lord Almighty, and that the final day of judgment will come.

1. What images come to your mind when you hear the term "thhat great and dreadful day of the LORD"?

Read Malachi 3:13–4:6.

2. How would you describe the sin of the people (3:13-15)?

◆ **3.** Under what circumstances are you likely to speak against God?

At those times, what do you think or say?

4. What positive response did some of the people make (3:16)?

5. In what ways will the Lord separate the righteous and the wicked?

6. How does God's judgment uphold his policy of justice?

♦ **7.** What does it mean to fear or revere the Lord (3:16; 4:2)?

8. How would it feel to be one of God's righteous ones (3:16–4:6)?

♦ **9.** God says that in preparing his people for his coming, the prophet Elijah will turn the hearts of parents and children toward each other. From your experience, what would be the results of such a shift in relationships?

10. What would you have to do to enable this healing to occur in your family? (Consider your parents as well as your children.)

11. Review the entire book of Malachi jottting down all the characteristics of God you find. Then discuss the following questions.

a) Is there something on this list you have not considered before?

b) Are there any items on the list that make you uncomfortable? Why?

c) What part of this picture of God means most to you right now? Why?

12. With this list in mind, spend a few minutes in prayer together, thanking and praising God.

THE LIVING GOD

Jonah, Habakkuk, and Malachi

Though Jonah, Habakkuk, and Malachi lived at different times and faced different situations, in all of their writings we have met the living God and have seen various aspects of his character. The composite picture of God that these three prophets have given us is encouraging. We serve a great, merciful God who indeed reigns over all.

♦ **Divide into three small groups, assigning one book for each to cover. Search out answers to the following three questions. At the end of the small group study time (about 20 minutes), come back to the large group and discuss your findings.**

　　1. How do you see God's love being expressed toward those who belong to him? (Look for specific actions and words.)

2. What arouses God's wrath?

3. Why is it important to have a God who cares about justice?

Summary questions for all.

4. Having read Jonah, Habakkuk, and Malachi, what can you tell a friend about God and what he desires for our lives?

5. What would it mean for us to live responsibly?

6. From what we've learned, what response are you ready to make to God?

LEADER'S NOTES

■ Study 1/Running Away

Note on Jonah. Jonah was a prophet in Israel during the eighth century B.C. Nineveh was the capital city of the powerful nation of Assyria, a long-time enemy of Israel. Jonah was probably written sometime around 785–760 B.C., before Israel was conquered by Assyria in 722 B.C.

Question 3. Jonah goes to the largest seaport on the coast and buys a ticket to Tarshish, a city probably located to the west of Israel, across the Mediterranean Sea in the south of Spain. This was in the opposite direction of Nineveh which was located northeast of Israel. Use a Bible map to find the places mentioned.

Question 8. What we do reveals what we really believe. The sailors' actions were more consistent with their beliefs than Jonah's were with his beliefs.

■ Study 2/Getting Caught

Note on Jonah 2. People sometimes discount the historicity of Jonah because of the "impossibility" of a man being swallowed by a large ish. We know Jonah was a real person (2 Kings 14:25), and until recently both Jews and Christians have regarded this book as a record of actual fact. Jesus clearly thought these events really occurred (Matthew 12:40-41). There are a number of sea creatures able to swallow a man, and the Princeton Theological Review (1927) refers to an actual case. The presence of miracle in a story does not mean it was not intended to be accepted as an historical account. However, whether we believe this to be an allegory or to be history, the point of the story remains the same: God is a righteous but merciful God, deeply concerned with the repentance of men. It is not important in your discussion to settle the question of history versus allegory. Help your group avoid the "scientific" arguments in favor of discussing the more important meaning of the passage.

Question 7. It is important to emphasize Jonah's conclusion that God is the only way out: "Salvation comes from the Lord" (Jonah 2:9).

Question 13. This is an opportunity for group members to witness to their experience of God's tender care in turning their hard experiences into vehicles for welding strong bonds with him. Sharing these can be an encouragement to each other and a witness to non-Christians in the group.

■ Study 3/Responding to God

Question 2. This question should promote a search through the whole chapter. Find evidences of the social, economic, political, moral, and cultural climates of Nineveh.

Question 7. *Repentance* is more than feeling sorry for what you have done. It includes turning away from those actions and going in another direction. Here the people heard God's word, believed it, admitted their sin, felt sorry and afraid, turned away from evil, and acted in a way that showed their change of heart.

Question 10. Jonah 3:10 shows God relenting. This doesn't mean that God is capricious and changeable, but that he is merciful and longs to see us turn to him. Several Scripture passages refer to this idea of God relenting and having compassion on those who turn to him. (See Jeremiah 18:6-10 and Joel 2:12-14.)

■ Study 4/Showing Anger

Question 7. Here, as throughout the book, God was interested in revealing sin so that repentance and healing could begin. The plan was to expose Jonah to his own self-centeredness. He didn't pity either people or animals, but only himself in his own momentary discomfort. He only felt sorry for things that were useful to him (the vine).

Question 9. God does not reveal his will in one way only. A thorough knowledge of his character and purpose as revealed in the Bible is our best guide. However, as this book shows, he verifies his will and makes it more explicit in a variety of different ways.

■ Study 5/Learning to See with God's Perspective

Note on Habakkuk. Habakkuk was written sometime around 612–588 B.C., just before Judah, the southern kingdom, was taken over by Babylon in 588 B.C. The name *Habakkuk* comes from a Hebrew word meaning "to clasp" or "embrace." An *oracle* (Habakkuk 1:1) is a prophetic utterance, almost synonymous with *revelation* (adapted from the *New Bible Commentary: Revised,* pp. 767–769. Grand Rapids, Mich.: Eerdmans, 1970).

Question 12. *Revelation* in Habakkuk 2:2 is another term for God's Word.

Study 6/Learning to Live in a Mixed-up World

Question 4. This question helps explore the practical meaning of the phrase "the righteous will live by his faith." The believing person of faith is able to live, in the fullest sense of the word, enjoying the favor of God's presence, with or without material benefits. Note also the contrast between the pride and arrogance of the wicked and living by faith and dependence on God.

Question 5. If your group has trouble with the modern-day equivalents, here is one for each section to prime the pump. Be sure to get others from the group.

1. Depending on credit cards.
2. False reporting on medical insurance that jeopardizes others' credit.
3. Urban landlords' sharp rent practices.
4. Cutting and degrading remarks.
5. Trusting financial investments for security.

Question 9. Sharing can be time consuming. Limit descriptions to two or three sentences. If members of your group are uncomfortable praying aloud, have each person pray silently for the one on his or her right.

Study 7/Learning to Rejoice in God's Salvation

Note on Habakkuk 3:1. *Shigionoth* was probably a literary or musical term. This prayer was a song. See also the *Selah*s and the instruction at the end—all are notations for a song or liturgy.

60

Question 3. Compare with the earlier passages in Habakkuk 1:2-3, 12; 2:1)

Question 4. *Teman* and *Mt. Paran* (Habakkuk 3:3) were two place associated with early Israelite history, probably used here to sym bolize that God had been with his people in a special way since their beginning as a nation. *Cushan* (verse 3:7) is an archaic name for the land of Midian. The Midianites led Israel into idolatry.

Question 5. God's actions have both general and specific results. His power and glory, for instance, may be made evident in a broad way by his mighty acts, but the same acts may also be specifically for the purpose of saving his people (as in Habakkuk 3:13).

■ Study 8/Worshiping the Lord Almighty

Note on Malachi. Malachi was written to the Jews in Jerusalem sometime around 430 B.C., after they had returned from seventy years of exile in Babylon. As in Habakkuk, an *oracle* is a divinely authorized communication. *Malachi* means "my messenger."

Question 2. God refers to Israel's history here. Jacob and Esau were twin sons of Isaac, and the brothers were rivals even in their mother's womb. Jacob was the forefather of the nation of Israel, and Esau founded the great nation of Edom. (See Genesis 25:21-34; 27:1-46; 36:1-8). The Edomite nation was the sworn enemy of its brother nation, Israel. Edom's rebellion and hatred of Israel is recounted in Ezekiel 25:12-14; 35:3-15 and Amos 1:11-12.

Question 3. God's mercy to Israel, even though they had sinned, proved his love. Esau (Edom) was Israel's enemy, and its destruction showed that God cared about Israel and would defend them against their enemies.

Study 9/Living in Faithfulness

Question 4. The descendants of Levi and Aaron became the priests for the nation of Israel (1 Chronicles 23:24-32). The original covenant of life and peace mentioned in Malachi 2:5 can be found in Numbers 25:10-13. In Malachi 2:5-7, the nature of true priestly service is laid out. It is clear from these verses that the covenant promised prosperity in return for true reverence.

Question 8. The Bible often uses marriage as a close analogy for God's relationship (as a husband) to his people (as wife or bride). Find the parallels suggested by Malachi.

Question 9. God desires godly offspring not only physically but spiritually for a continuing witness. The fruit of the Spirit is the product of a relationship with God, just as faithful children are a product of a marriage between two of his people.

Question 10. The word *garment* in Malachi 2:16 can be understood to stand for the marriage relationship, since when a man claimed a woman as his wife he cast his garment over her (Ruth 3:9). The reference here is to the brutal treatment involved in divorce.

Study 10/Returning to God

Question 3. A refiner burns away all impurities in a metal until it shines like a mirror. Gold that has been refined is reduced to a pure state; it is "pure gold."

Question 11. Question 11 searches out the statements in the passage that express God's desires for his people. Question 12 relates these desires to each individual's needs.

■ Study 11/Waiting for His Coming

Question 3. Each of us is tempted at various times to feel displeased with the way God is handling things. This question is to help us become aware of our own weak spots. Perhaps we don't actively rebel against God, but our thoughts and words give us away.

Question 7. To fear or revere the Lord means to have a reverential awe and respect for God.

Question 9. In Malachi 4:5 there is a reference to Elijah, who was an important prophet in the past history of the Hebrew people. Jesus later indicated that the prophecy in these verses referred to the ministry of John the Baptist. (See Matthew 11:13-14; 17:11-13.)

■ Study 12/The Living God

Note to Leader: Your own careful study of each of these books in answering the study questions will be a big help to you in leading this discussion. Write the answers with the verse references where you found them. When you have a list for each book, group similar answers together and summarize your findings. In the group discussion, probably your most important job will be to watch the time and keep things moving, both in the small groups and in the larger discussion, so all the questions are handled and everyone is able to have a complete overview of the teaching of these three books.

WHAT SHOULD WE STUDY NEXT?

To help your group answer that question, we've listed the Fisher-man Guides by category so you can choose your next study.

TOPICAL STUDIES

Becoming Women of Purpose, Barton

Building Your House on the Lord, Brestin

Discipleship, Reapsome

Doing Justice, Showing Mercy, Wright

Encouraging Others, Johnson

Examining the Claims of Jesus, Brestin

Friendship, Brestin

The Fruit of the Spirit, Briscoe

Great Doctrines of the Bible, Board

Great Passages of the Bible, Plueddemann

Great People of the Bible, Plueddemann

Great Prayers of the Bible, Plueddemann

Growing Through Life's Challenges, Reapsome

Guidance & God's Will, Stark

Higher Ground, Brestin

How Should a Christian Live? (1,2, & 3 John), Brestin

Marriage, Stevens

Moneywise, Larsen

One Body, One Spirit, Larsen

The Parables of Jesus, Hunt

Prayer, Jones

The Prophets, Wright

Proverbs & Parables, Brestin

Relationships, Hunt

Satisfying Work, Stevens & Schoberg

Senior Saints, Reapsome

Sermon on the Mount, Hunt

The Ten Commandments, Briscoe

When Servants Suffer, Rhodes

Who Is Jesus? Van Reken

Worship, Sibley

BIBLE BOOK STUDIES

Genesis, Fromer & Keyes

Job, Klug

Psalms, Klug

Proverbs: Wisdom That Works, Wright

Ecclesiastes, Brestin

Jonah, Habakkuk, & Malachi, Fromer & Keyes

Matthew, Sibley

Mark, Christensen

Luke, Keyes

John: Living Word, Kuniholm

Acts 1-12, Christensen

Paul (Acts 13-28), Christensen

Romans: The Christian Story, Reapsome

1 Corinthians, Hummel

Strengthened to Serve (2 Corinthians), Plueddemann

Galatians, Titus & Philemon, Kuniholm

Ephesians, Baylis

Philippians, Klug

Colossians, Shaw

Letters to the Thessalonians, Fromer & Keyes

Letters to Timothy, Fromer & Keyes

Hebrews, Hunt

James, Christensen

1 & 2 Peter, Jude, Brestin

How Should a Christian Live? (1, 2 & 3 John), Brestin

Revelation, Hunt

BIBLE CHARACTER STUDIES

Ruth & Daniel, Stokes

David: Man after God's Own Heart, Castleman

Job, Klug

King David: Trusting God for a Lifetime, Castleman

Elijah, Castleman

Men Like Us, Heidebrecht & Scheuermann

Peter, Castleman

Paul (Acts 13-28), Christensen

Great People of the Bible, Plueddemann

Women Like Us, Barton

Women Who Achieved for God, Christensen

Women Who Believed God, Christensen